What Was It Like During Christmas in the 90s?

A Journal to Revisit and Share the 90s Holiday Vibe

~ Riya Aarini ~

What Was It Like During Christmas in the 90s?
A Journal to Revisit and Share the 90s Holiday Vibe
Text Copyright © 2025 by Riya Aarini

ISBN: 978-1-956496-64-2 (paperback)
ISBN: 978-1-956496-65-9 (hardcover)

This book belongs to '90s kid

_____

_____

Contents

Merry Christmas

Welcome to Your '90s Christmases!

Christmases in the '90s hold meaningful places in many hearts. Fewer things existed back then, from toys to television shows. As a result, everything about the seasons felt extra special.

People enjoyed a closeness without smartphones competing for attention. Gifts were more personal, as shopping was bravely done at overcrowded malls rather than online with one click.

The decade's strings of Christmas lights are equally memorable, with their soft glows subtly evoking the magic of the season. Despite the need to replace incandescent bulbs frequently, the warm '90s holiday lights surpass today's most spectacular LED lighting.

Christmas nostalgia remains strong for '90s kids. Take a festive trip down memory lane as you fill out the answers to these prompts and relive the joyous Christmases of your childhood!

Christmas Tree

Did the magic of Christmas officially start once the tree was up?

How soon before Christmas did your family set up the holiday tree?

Did your family prefer a live or an artificial Christmas tree?
If a live tree, where did you get it from?

If an artificial tree, how much did it cost?

In what room did your family put up the holiday tree?

How did you decorate in the '90s? Garlands, silver tinsel, strings of lights?

If tinsel was a part of your tree decorations, did you go all out covering the tree (and home) with the sparkly strands?

Describe a cherished holiday ornament.

Were any holiday ornaments passed down from prior generations? If so, describe one and its significance.

Did you craft holiday ornaments? If so, describe one.

Express how it felt to hang your handcrafted Christmas ornaments on the tree.

Who held the honor of topping the Christmas tree with the star?

How long after Christmas did your family keep the tree up?

What did you do with the Christmas tree once the holiday season ended?

Holiday Home
Decorations

How did your family decorate the home's exterior for Christmas in the '90s?

Did your family create handmade decorations for the front lawn? If so, describe one.

Did you and your family drive through neighborhoods to admire homes lit up for Christmas? If so, describe the sights and your sense of awe.

Christmas Shopping

Did you scour through print holiday catalogs to find Christmas gifts you liked to receive or give?

Did you write a Christmas wish list, noting the catalog page numbers?

How early did you start your Christmas shopping?

How much time did you or your family spend at the mall shopping for Christmas gifts?

How crowded did the malls get during the holiday shopping seasons?

Describe any mall-related fiascos (like splitting up or getting lost in the sea of shoppers).

How impressive were the toy stores/sections in the '90s?

Did bands play Christmas music live at the malls? If so, did you enjoy the experience?

Did your mall hold shows with animatronic Christmas figures? If so, how spectacular were they?

Describe how your mall was decorated for Christmas.

Did it take all day to hunt for a specific gift? Did the challenge of finding the right gift lend extra magic to the season?

How many times did your family circle the mall parking lot to find a parking space?

How well did you time gift purchases to receive them before Christmas, considering shipping took weeks in the '90s?

Despite the frenzy, did mall shopping inspire a sense of comfort and community—unlike shopping online today?

Did you enjoy the hustle and bustle of Christmas shopping in the '90s?

Did your Christmas gifts come with stories, such as having to drive fifty miles through snow and ice, only to find the store had none left in stock? If so, tell one story.

Christmas Gifts

Giving holiday gifts in the '90s required an investment in thought and effort, especially since shipping took forever and gifts didn't arrive wrapped. As a result, gift-giving had heart!

Name five dream Christmas presents you received in the '90s.

_____

_____

_____

_____

_____

Did you ever receive a lump of coal? If so, why?

List three gifts you found in your Christmas stockings.

_____

_____

_____

Describe a handmade Christmas gift you received in the '90s.

Did you ever ask Santa for a gift and didn't receive it? How did you justify that?

Did you ever catch your parents sneaking gifts under the holiday tree on Christmas Eve? If so, what emotions ran through you?

Explain how you caught them. Camcorder, in person?

Did you ever find receipts for the Christmas gifts you received, introducing doubts about the existence of Santa Claus?

Do you think people gave fewer Christmas gifts during the '90s, making giving and receiving gifts more exquisite experiences?

Did receiving Christmas presents in the '90s hold greater meaning? If so, how?

Santa Claus

How old were you when you first learned about Santa Claus?

Who first explained Santa Claus to you?

What emotions ran through you when you discovered Santa brought toys and joys every Christmas?

How magical did Santa feel to you?

Did you visit Santa? If so, where? Common places included the mall, Christmas-themed amusement parks, and winter wonderlands.

What emotions did the meeting with Santa inspire?

What did you think of Santa upon meeting him?

Did you take home a photo of Santa and you? If so, describe the photo.

Do you still have this photo?

Did you write letters to Santa Claus? If so, what did you ask for?

Did you mail the letters to the North Pole? If so, describe the envelope, Santa's address, and from where you mailed it.

Did you wait up to get a peek at Santa leaving gifts under the Christmas tree? If so, how late did you stay up?

Did you ever catch Santa in action?

Did you leave Santa cookies and milk on Christmas Eve? If not, what did you leave him?

Were the snacks gone by Christmas morning?

Until what age did you believe in Santa Claus?

Explain how you learned the truth about Santa Claus.

Did your world shatter?

Santa's Elves

Did you believe in Santa's elves?

Until what age did the fascination for the toy-making elves continue?

Santa's Reindeer

How did you learn about Santa's reindeer? Christmas TV specials, holiday stories, Christmas songs, holiday décor?

Growing up, did you memorize the names of Santa's nine reindeer?

Who was your favorite reindeer? Why?

Did you ever stay out on Christmas Eve, gazing at the sky to look for Santa's team of flying reindeer?

What did you believe gave Santa's reindeer the ability to fly? Magic dust, belief in Santa, special food, or something else?

Holiday Books

List your five favorite childhood Christmas books.

_____

_____

_____

_____

_____

Did your family read them to you? If so, describe the story time environment, such as next to the warmth of a crackling fireplace or while cozily tucked in bed.

What stories left an impression on you?

Who were your most beloved characters? What about them appealed to you?

Christmas Poems

Clement Clark Moore's "A Visit from St. Nicholas," also known as "'Twas the Night Before Christmas," with its snappy rhythm, left a memorable mark on many.

What Christmas poem captivated you most as a '90s kid?

Did you recite this poem as a Christmas tradition?

Christmas Movies

Top Christmas movie picks included
1992: "The Muppet Christmas Carol"
1993: "The Nightmare Before Christmas"
1998: "Jack Frost"

What were your favorite '90s Christmas movies?

Which movie best described Christmas in the '90s?

Where did you watch Christmas movies? At home on a VCR, in the theater, elsewhere?

With whom did you watch Christmas movies?

Did you rewatch Christmas movies in the '90s? If so, which ones, and how often?

If the nostalgia is strong, do you rewatch your beloved childhood Christmas movies today?

Christmas TV Specials

Well-liked holiday specials included "It's Christmastime Again Charlie Brown,"
"A Garfield Christmas Special," and "A Muppet Family Christmas."

What were your favorite Christmas TV specials in the '90s?

Did you refer to the "TV Guide" schedule to ensure you didn't miss the specials—since they aired once annually?

Did your family watch the Christmas specials together? What feelings did these times inspire?

What '90s Christmas commercials do you remember fondly?

Christmas Parades

Did you attend Christmas parades or watch them on TV?

If so, describe the sights, sounds, and magic of the holiday parades.

What were your favorite parts? Floats, Santa, live performances?

Express what it was like to watch the Christmas tree lighting.

Christmas Carols

Did you sing Christmas carols in the '90s? If so, with whom? Family, choir, professional carolers, Girl Scout troop?

Did you go house-to-house, singing carols? If so, describe the experience.

List three beloved Christmas carols.

_____

_____

_____

Christmas Music

Holiday tunes that topped the charts included

1994: "All I Want for Christmas Is You" by Mariah Carey

1996: "The Chanukah Song" by Adam Sandler

1999: "I Saw Mama Kissing Santa Claus" by Reba McEntire

List your top '90s Christmas song picks.

Christmas Theater

Visiting the theater was a popular holiday tradition for many during the '90s. Theatrical productions with themes of hope, goodwill, and peace were must-sees, bringing people together in the spirit of Christmas.

Did your family see "The Nutcracker"? If so, describe the sights, sounds, and feelings the classical ballet stirred up.

Did you see an adaptation of "A Christmas Carol"? If so, where?

Which characters fascinated you most?

Holiday Train Rides

Did you take holiday train rides in the '90s? If so, where?

Did the rides instill a sense of wonder and magic in you?

How memorable were the holiday train rides?

Holiday Sleigh Rides

Did you take sleigh rides through the snow?

Describe the enchantment of being pulled through the snow.

Sensory Experiences

Christmases in the '90s conjured up distinct aromas, sights, sounds, feels, and tastes.

Aromas

What were some unique scents of Christmas? The smell of pine needles, cloves and nutmeg from freshly baked gingerbread cookies...

Sights

What were some of the unforgettable sights of Christmas in the '90s? The soft glows of holiday lights, the decorated street posts...

Sounds

What sounds of '90s Christmases do you recall? The jingle of bells, the crunching of boots through the snow...

Feels

Describe the unforgettable feels of Christmas in the '90s. The cozy holiday sweaters, the biting cold...

Tastes

List the irresistible flavors of Christmas in the '90s. Peppermint candy canes, mint chocolates...

Flashes from the '90s Christmases Past

Flashes from the '90s
Christmases Past

Gingerbread Houses

Did you build gingerbread houses? If so, did your family make the dough from scratch?

List the '90s candies you used to decorate the gingerbread houses.

Holiday Window Displays

Did your family take strolls through town to admire the holiday window displays?

Describe one window display that stood out.

Christmas Vacations

How did you spend Christmas vacations in the '90s?

Did your family travel? If so, to what holiday destinations?

Christmas Plays

Did you participate in a Christmas play?

If so, what character did you play?

Describe one memorable costume.

Holiday Cookies

Popular Christmas cookies included candy cane cookies, shortbread cookies, and classic thumbprint cookies. The tasty morsels symbolized thankfulness, sharing, and togetherness.

Describe your favorite store-bought holiday cookies.

Did you bake holiday cookies? If so, was it a family holiday tradition?

Christmas Eve

How did you spend Christmas Eve in the '90s?

Did you feel excitement, longing, or anticipation on Christmas Eve, knowing the next morning you'd wake up to new gifts?

Christmas Day

How did you spend Christmas Day in the '90s?

Did you follow any Christmas traditions? If so, describe one.

Christmas Breakfasts/Brunches

Did your family prepare Christmas breakfasts or brunches? If so, what foods did they whip up?

Describe one of your best '90s holiday breakfast memories.

Christmas Dinners

Did your family prepare homemade Christmas dinners? What foods did they cook?

Did you prefer homemade stuffing and gravy over boxed or store-bought variations?

Did your family hold Christmas potlucks or buffets? If so, what dishes did friends and family bring?

What were your favorite Christmas dinner menu items?

Christmas Desserts

Sweet holiday treats included Yule log cakes, fruitcakes, Christmas tiramisu, and gelatin molds.

What Christmas desserts did you look forward to?

What was your opinion of fruitcakes, which received a bad rap in the '90s?

Did you regift the notoriously dry fruitcakes in the '90s?

If so, how many times did the fruitcakes pass through your social circle before being discarded?

Christmas Parties

Did your school throw Christmas parties? If so, what activities did you enjoy?

Did your family hold Christmas parties? If so, describe the festive '90s outfits.

Long-Distance
Holiday Greetings

The cost of long-distance calls in the '90s rose to astronomical heights. During peak hours, like Christmas, the price grew exponentially higher.

Did your family make long-distance telephone calls on Christmas? If so, how expensive did the calls get?

Who did you call long-distance during Christmas?

Did you ship Christmas presents internationally? If so, how long did they take to reach?

Social Interactions

Do you feel people interacted more authentically during Christmas in the '90s (when smartphones didn't consume their attention)?

Did you feel a greater bond with people, even strangers, on Christmas in the '90s?

White Christmases

Did you enjoy white Christmases in the '90s?

If snow was abundant in your area, what winter activities did you participate in? Building snowmen, sledding, making snow angels, building snow forts, snowball fights?

How magical did it feel to drive through Christmas snow?

Charities and Volunteering

Did you or your family give to charity during Christmas in the '90s? If so, to which one?

Did you volunteer during the holidays in the '90s? If so, where?

Christmas Intangibles

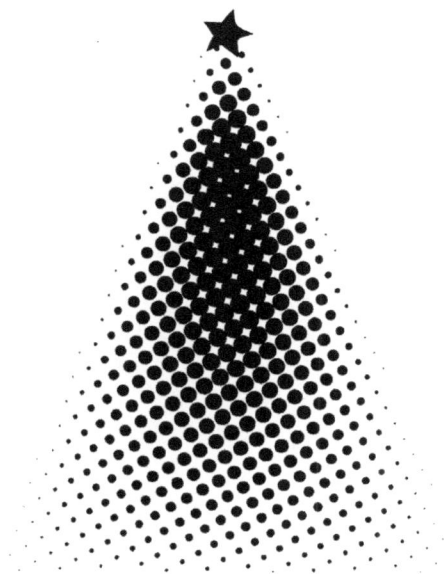

On Christmas Day in the '90s, shops closed, and people welcomed the opportunity to spend time with loved ones.

Did you consider Father Time on your side during Christmas in the '90s? In other words, did time move at a slower pace, allowing you to savor the moments of the season?

Do you feel greater anticipation filled Christmases in the '90s, in comparison to today where nearly everything, from toys to movies, is available on-demand?

Do you feel Christmas was simpler in the '90s? If so, how?

If you awoke early on Christmas morning, did a profound sense of peace and quiet greet you?

Do you feel Christmas in the '90s held greater sanctity?

Describe your most memorable '90s Christmas.

What was the true meaning of Christmas for you in the '90s?

More Flashes from the '90s Christmases Past

More Flashes from the '90s Christmases Past

Here's to an Unforgettable '90s Christmas!

Christmastime in the '90s remains near and dear to those privileged to have once been a part of these simpler times. Perhaps it's because the merry seasons were a part of their carefree childhood, or maybe it's because '90s Christmases abounded with irreplicable qualities.

As '90s kids reminiscence and recreate their beloved traditions, the '90s Christmas vibes live on!

Books in the
What Was It Like series

What Was It Like Growing Up in the 70s?
A Journal to Revisit and Share the Groovy 70s

What Was It Like Growing Up in the 80s?
A Journal to Revisit and Share the Totally Awesome 80s

What Was It Like Fooding in the 80s?
A Journal to Revisit and Share 80s Totally Tubular Eats

What Was It Like During Christmas in the 80s?
A Journal to Revisit and Share the 80s Holiday Spirit

What Was It Like Growing Up in the 90s?
A Journal to Revisit and Share the Rad 90s

What Was It Like Marrying in the 90s?
A Journal (for Her) to Revisit and Share 90s Wedding
Magic

www.ingramcontent.com/pod-product-compliance
Lightning Source LLC
Chambersburg PA
CBHW052022030426
42335CB00026B/3251